the Seven-Day Scriptural Rosary

Larry London

Our Sunday Visitor Publishing Division
Our Sunday Visitor, Inc.
Huntington, Indiana 46750

Nihil Obstat
Rev. John A Najdowski, Chancellor
Censor Librorum

Imprimatur
✝Joseph F. Breitenbeck, D.D.
Bishop of Grand Rapids
November 15, 1988

Our Sunday Visitor Publishing Division
Our Sunday Visitor, Inc.
200 Noll Plaza
Huntington, Indiana 46750

International Standard Book No.: 0-87973-524-4
Library of Congress Catalog Card No.: 88-63552

*Cover design & illustrations by Steve Windmiller;
rosary illustration on page 127 by Constance London*

Published in the United States of America
524

Preface: The Purpose of the Seven-Day Scriptural Rosary

Our Mother Mary has long been a great source of strength, guidance, and consolation to me, as she has been to countless other people. The Holy Spirit led me to the Catholic Church mainly through the Sacred Scriptures, and so I have found praying the Scriptures with our Blessed Mother quite natural.

Mary wants so very much to reveal her Son's ways to us, and what better way than through his Word? I have found meditating on appropriate Scripture while praying the rosary to be a double blessing: first, a blessing from spending time with Mary, who is such a perfect model for us; and second, from a greater understanding and faith that comes from meditating on the Word of God.

The Seven-Day Scriptural Rosary

reveals much more of our Lord's and his Blessed Mother's lives than does the commonly prayed rosary. My hope and prayer is that, through your praying the rosary and meditating on these mysteries, you will come to deeper faith and greater love for our Lord and our Blessed Mother.

Explanation and Plan of the Seven-Day Scriptural Rosary

The distinguishing feature of the Seven-Day Scriptural Rosary is that there is a unique set of five rosary mysteries for each day of the week. There are a total of three hundred fifty Scripture excerpts for meditation. One is read before each Hail Mary over the course of the week, fifty each day of the week. Five of the total thirty-five rosary mysteries are prayed each day. Each mystery contains ten Hail Marys along with the corresponding Scripture meditation, and so we have a Rosarium — fifty hail Marys — prayed each day.

Below are listed the recommended mysteries for each day of the week.

Monday — **THE JOYFUL MYSTERIES** • p. 6

Tuesday — **THE SALVATION MYSTERIES** • p. 25

Wednesday — **THE HEALING MYSTERIES** • p. 41

Thursday — **THE EUCHARISTIC MYSTERIES** • p. 57

Friday — **THE SORROWFUL MYSTERIES** • p. 73

Saturday — **THE CONSOLING MYSTERIES** • p. 89

Sunday — **THE GLORIOUS MYSTERIES** • p. 107

An appendix with the prayers and method of the rosary can be found on pages 125-128.

FIRST JOYFUL MYSTERY

The Annunciation

☆ *Our Father* ☆

The angel Gabriel was sent from God
   . . . to a virgin . . . /

and the virgin's name was Mary.

Luke 1:26-27

☆*Hail Mary*☆

And coming to her, he said, /
    "Hail, favored one! The Lord is with
      you."

Luke 1:28

☆*Hail Mary*☆

But she was greatly troubled at what was
    said /
  and pondered what sort of greeting
    this might be.

Luke 1:29

☆*Hail Mary*☆

Then the angel said to her, /
    "Do not be afraid, Mary, for you have
    found favor with God."

Luke 1:30

☆*Hail Mary*☆

"Behold, you will conceive in your

womb and bear a son, /
and you shall name him Jesus."

Luke 1:31

☆*Hail Mary*☆

"He will be great and will be called Son
of the Most High, /
and the Lord God will give him the
throne of David his father. . . ."

Luke 1:32

☆*Hail Mary*☆

"And he will rule over the house of
Jacob forever, /
and of his kingdom there will be no
end."

Luke 1:33

☆*Hail Mary*☆

But Mary said to the angel, /
"How can this be, since I have no
relations with a man?"

Luke 1:34

☆*Hail Mary*☆

"The holy Spirit will come upon you,
and the power of the Most High
will overshadow you. /
Therefore the child to be born will be
called holy, the Son of God."

Luke 1:35

☆*Hail Mary*☆

Mary said, "Behold, I am the handmaid
of the Lord. /
May it be done to me according to
your word."

Luke 1:38

☆*Hail Mary*☆
☆*Glory Be*☆

SECOND JOYFUL MYSTERY

The Visitation

☆*Our Father*☆

Mary set out and traveled to the hill
country in haste to a town of
Judah, /
where she entered the house of
Zechariah and greeted Elizabeth.

Luke 1:39-40

☆*Hail Mary*☆

When Elizabeth heard Mary's greeting, /
the infant leaped in her womb. . .

Luke 1:41

☆*Hail Mary*☆

Elizabeth, filled with the holy Spirit,
cried out in a loud voice and said, /
"Most blessed are you among women,

and blessed is the fruit of your
womb."

☆*Hail Mary*☆

"Blessed are you who believed /
that what was spoken to you by the
Lord would be fulfilled."

Luke 1:45
☆*Hail Mary*☆

And Mary said: "My soul proclaims the
greatness of the Lord; /
my spirit rejoices in God my savior."

Luke 1:46-47
☆*Hail Mary*☆

"For he has looked upon his handmaid's
lowliness; behold from now on will
all ages call me blessed. /
The Mighty One has done great things
for me, and holy is his name."

Luke 1:48-49
☆*Hail Mary*☆

"His mercy is from age to age /
    to those who fear him."

Luke 1:50

☆Hail Mary☆

"He has shown might with his arm,
    dispersed the arrogant of mind and
    heart. /
He has thrown down the rulers from
    their thrones but lifted up the
    lowly."

Luke 1:51-52

☆Hail Mary☆

"The hungry he has filled with good
    things; /
the rich he has sent away empty."

Luke 1:53

☆Hail Mary☆

"He has helped Israel his servant,
    remembering his mercy, /
according to his promise to our

fathers, to Abraham and to his
descendants forever."

Luke 1:54,55

☆*Hail Mary*☆
☆*Glory Be*☆

THIRD JOYFUL MYSTERY

The Nativity

☆*Our Father*☆

"Behold, the virgin shall be with child
and bear a son, /
and they shall name him Emmanuel,"
which means "God is with us."
Matthew 1:23; cf. Is 7:14
☆*Hail Mary*☆

And Joseph too went up from Galilee
. . . to the city of David that is
called Bethlehem, /
to be enrolled with Mary, his
betrothed, who was with child.
Luke 2:4,5
☆*Hail Mary*☆

While they were there, the time came for
her to have her child, /

and she gave birth to her firstborn son.

Luke 2:6-7

☆*Hail Mary*☆

She wrapped him in swaddling clothes
    and laid him in a manger, /
because there was no room for them in
    the inn.

Luke 2:7

☆*Hail Mary*☆

Now there were shepherds in that region
    living in the fields. . . . /
The angel of the Lord appeared to
    them and the glory of the Lord
    shone around them.

Luke 2:8-9

☆*Hail Mary*☆

The angel said to them, "Do not be
    afraid; /
for behold, I proclaim to you good
    news of great joy that will be for all

the people."

Luke 2:10

☆*Hail Mary*☆

"For today in the city of David a savior
has been born for you /
who is Messiah and Lord."

Luke 2:11

☆*Hail Mary*☆

Behold, magi from the east arrived. . . . /
They prostrated themselves and did
him homage.

Matthew 2:1,11

☆*Hail Mary*☆

"Glory to God in the highest /
and on earth peace to those on whom
his favor rests."

Luke 2:14

☆*Hail Mary*☆

And the Word became flesh and made
his dwelling among us, /

and we saw his glory, the glory as of
the Father's only Son, full of grace
and truth.

John 1:14

☆*Hail Mary*☆
☆*Glory Be*☆

FOURTH JOYFUL MYSTERY

The Presentation

☆*Our Father*☆

They took him up to Jerusalem to
    present him to the Lord . . . /
and to offer the sacrifice. . . .

Luke 2:22,24

☆*Hail Mary*☆

Now there was a man in Jerusalem
    whose name was Simeon. /
. . . and the holy spirit was upon him.

Luke 2:25

☆*Hail Mary*☆

He came in the Spirit into the temple; /
. . . he took him into his arms and
    blessed God. . . .

Luke 2:27,28

☆*Hail Mary*☆

"Now, Master, you may let your servant
go in peace, /
according to your word. . ."

Luke 2:29

☆*Hail Mary*☆

"For my eyes have seen your salvation, /
which you prepared in sight of all the
peoples . . ."

Luke 2:30-31

☆*Hail Mary*☆

"A light for revelation to the Gentiles, /
and glory for your people Israel."

Luke 2:32

☆*Hail Mary*☆

Simeon blessed them and said to Mary
his mother, /
"Behold, this child is destined for the
fall and rise of many in Israel, and
to be a sign that will be
contradicted"

Luke 2:34

☆*Hail Mary*☆

"(And you yourself a sword will pierce) /
so that the thoughts of many hearts
may be revealed."

Luke 2:35

☆*Hail Mary*☆

There was also a prophetess, Anna. . . . /
She never left the temple, but
worshipped night and day with
fasting and prayer.

Luke 2:36,37

☆*Hail Mary*☆

And coming forward at that very time,
she gave thanks to God /
and spoke about the child to all who
were awaiting the redemption of
Jerusalem.

Luke 2:38

☆*Hail Mary*☆
☆*Glory Be*☆

FIFTH JOYFUL MYSTERY

The Finding of Jesus in the Temple

☆*Our Father*☆

Each year his parents went to Jerusalem
   for the feast of Passover, /
and when he was twelve years old,
   they went up according to festival
   custom.

Luke 2:41-42

☆*Hail Mary*☆

After they had completed its days, as
   they were returning, /
the boy Jesus remained behind in
   Jerusalem, but his parents did not
   know it.

Luke 2:43

☆*Hail Mary*☆

Thinking that he was in the caravan,

they journeyed for a day /
and looked for him among their
relatives and acquaintances . . .

                              Luke 2:44

☆*Hail Mary*☆

But not finding him, they returned to
Jerusalem to look for him. /
After three days they found him in the
temple. . . .

                           Luke 2:45,46

☆*Hail Mary*☆

Sitting in the midst of the teachers,
listening to them and asking them
questions, /
and all who heard him were astounded
at his understanding and his
answers.

                           Luke 2:46-47

☆*Hail Mary*☆

His mother said to him, "Son, why have
you done this to us? /

Your father and I have been looking
for you with great anxiety."

Luke 2:48

☆*Hail Mary*☆

He said to them, "Why were you looking
for me? /
Did you not know that I must be in
my Father's house?"

Luke 2:49

☆*Hail Mary*☆

But they did not understand /
what he said to them.

Luke 2:50

☆*Hail Mary*☆

He went down with them and came to
Nazareth, and was obedient to
them; /
and his mother kept all these things in
her heart.

Luke 2:51

☆*Hail Mary*☆

And Jesus advanced [in] wisdom and age
and favor /
before God and man.

Luke 2:52

☆Hail Mary☆
☆Glory Be☆

FIRST SALVATION MYSTERY

Jesus Teaches Nicodemus

☆*Our Father*☆

Now there was a Pharisee named
     Nicodemus. . . . He came to Jesus

at night and said to him, /

". . . no one can do these signs that
you are doing unless God is with
him."

John 3:1,2

☆*Hail Mary*☆

Jesus answered and said to him, "Amen,
amen, I say to you, /
no one can see the kingdom of God
without being born from above."

John 3:3

☆*Hail Mary*☆

Nicodemus said to him, "How can a
person once grown old be born
again? /
Surely he cannot reenter his mother's
womb and be born again, can he?"

John 3:4

☆*Hail Mary*☆

Jesus answered, "Amen, amen, I say to

you, no one can enter the kingdom
of God /
without being born of water and
Spirit." John 3:5

"What is born of flesh is flesh /
and what is born of spirit is spirit."

John 3:6

"The wind blows where it wills, and you
can hear the sound it makes, but
you do not know where it comes
from or where it goes; /
so it is with everyone who is born of
the Spirit."

John 3:8

"No one has gone up to heaven except
the one who has come down from
heaven, /
the Son of Man."

John 3:13

☆*Hail Mary*☆

"For God so loved the world that he
    gave his only Son, /
  so that everyone who believes in him
    might not perish but might have
    eternal life."

John 3:16

☆*Hail Mary*☆

"For God did not send his Son into the
    world to condemn the world, /
  but that the world might be saved
    through him."

John 3:17

☆*Hail Mary*☆

"Whoever believes in him will not be
    condemned, /
  but whoever does not believe has
    already been condemned. . . ."

John 3:18

☆*Hail Mary*☆
☆*Glory Be*☆

SECOND SALVATION MYSTERY

The Good Shepherd

☆*Our Father*☆

"Whoever does not enter a sheepfold
through the gate but climbs over
elsewhere /
is a thief and a robber."

John 10:1

☆*Hail Mary*☆

Jesus said again, "Amen, amen, I say to
you, /
I am the gate for the sheep."

John 10:7

☆*Hail Mary*☆

"I am the gate. Whoever enters through
me will be saved, /
and will come in and go out and find
pasture."

John 10:9

☆*Hail Mary*☆

"A thief comes only to steal and
    slaughter and destroy; /
 I came so that they might have life and
    have it more abundantly."

John 10:10

☆Hail Mary☆

"I am the good shepherd. /
 A good shepherd lays down his life for
    the sheep."

John 10:11

☆Hail Mary☆

"This is why the Father loves me, /
 because I lay down my life in order to
    take it up again."

John 10:17

☆Hail Mary☆

"I told you and you do not believe. /

The works I do in my Father's name
testify to me."

John 10:25

☆*Hail Mary*☆

"My sheep hear my voice; /
I know them, and they follow me."

John 10:27

☆*Hail Mary*☆

"I give them eternal life, and they shall
never perish. /
No one can take them out of my
hand."

John 10:28

☆*Hail Mary*☆

"The Father and I /
are one."

John 10:30

☆*Hail Mary*☆
☆*Glory Be*☆

THIRD SALVATION MYSTERY

The Rich Man

☆*Our Father*☆

A man ran up, knelt down before him,
and asked, /
"Good teacher, what must I do to
inherit eternal life?"

Mark 10:17

☆*Hail Mary*☆

Jesus answered him, "Why do you call
me good? /
No one is good but God alone."

Mark 10:18

☆*Hail Mary*☆

"You know the commandments: 'You
shall not kill; you shall not commit
adultery; /
you shall not steal; you shall not bear
false witness; you shall not defraud;

honor your father and your
mother.' "

Mark 10:19

☆*Hail Mary*☆

He replied and said to him, /
   "Teacher, all of these I have observed
      from my youth."

Mark 10:20

☆*Hail Mary*☆

Jesus, looking at him, loved him and said
     to him, /
   "You are lacking in one thing."

Mark 10:21

☆*Hail Mary*☆

"Go, sell what you have, and give to
   [the] poor and you will have
     treasure in heaven; /
then come, follow me."

Mark 10:21

☆*Hail Mary*☆

At that statement his face fell, and he
went away sad, /
   for he had many possessions.

Mark 10:22

☆Hail Mary☆

Jesus looked around and said to his
disciples, /
   "How hard it is for those who have
   wealth to enter the kingdom of
   God!"   Mark 10:23

☆Hail Mary☆

They were exceedingly astonished and
said among themselves, /
   "Then who can be saved?"

Mark 10:26

☆Hail Mary☆

"For human beings it is impossible, but
not for God. /
   All things are possible for God."

Mark 10:27

☆Hail Mary☆
☆Glory Be☆

FOURTH SALVATION MYSTERY

The Vine and the Branches

☆*Our Father*☆

"I am the true vine, /
   and my Father is the vine grower."

John 15:1

☆*Hail Mary*☆

"He takes away every branch in me that
      does not bear fruit, /
   and every one that does he prunes so
      that it bears more fruit."

John 15:2

☆*Hail Mary*☆

"Just as a branch cannot bear fruit on its
      own unless it remains on the vine, /
   so neither can you unless you remain
      in me."

John 15:4

"Whoever remains in me and I in him
     will bear much fruit, /
  because without me you can do
     nothing."

John 15:5

☆*Hail Mary*☆

"By this is my Father glorified, /
  that you bear much fruit and become
     my disciples."

John 15:8

☆*Hail Mary*☆

"If you keep my commandments, you
     will remain in my love, /
  just as I have kept my Father's
     commandments and remain in his
     love."

John 15:10

☆*Hail Mary*☆

"I have told you this so that my joy

might be in you /
and your joy might be complete."

John 15:11

☆*Hail Mary*☆

"This is my commandment: /
love one another as I love you."

John 15:12

☆*Hail Mary*☆

"No one has greater love than this, /
to lay down one's life for one's
friends."

John 15:13

☆*Hail Mary*☆

"You are my friends /
if you do what I command you."

John 15:14

☆*Hail Mary*☆
☆*Glory Be*☆

FIFTH SALVATION MYSTERY

The Judgment

☆*Our Father*☆

"When the Son of Man comes in his
　　glory . . . /
　all the nations will be assembled
　　before him."

Matthew 25:31,32

☆*Hail Mary*☆

"He will separate them one from
　　another, /
　as a shepherd separates the sheep from
　　the goats."

Matthew 25:32

☆*Hail Mary*☆

"He will place the sheep on his right /
　and the goats on his left."

Matthew 25:33

☆*Hail Mary*☆

"Then the King will say to those on his right, 'Come you who are blessed by my Father. /
Inherit the kingdom prepared for you from the foundation of the world.' "

Matthew 25:34

☆Hail Mary☆

" 'For I was hungry and you gave me food, I was thirsty and you gave me drink, /
a stranger and you welcomed me . . .' "

Matthew 25:35

☆Hail Mary☆

"Naked and you clothed me, ill and you cared for me, /
in prison and you visited me."

Matthew 25:36

☆Hail Mary☆

" 'Amen, I say to you, /   -

whatever you did for one of these least brothers of mine, you did for me.' "

Matthew 25:40

☆*Hail Mary*☆

"Then he will say to those on his left, 'Depart from me, you accursed, / into the eternal fire prepared for the devil and his angels.' "

Matthew 25:41

☆*Hail Mary*☆

"He will answer them, 'Amen, I say to you, / what you did not do for one of these least ones, you did not do for me.' "

Matthew 25:45

☆*Hail Mary*☆

"And these will go off to eternal punishment, / but the righteous to eternal life."

Matthew 25:46

☆*Hail Mary*☆
☆*Glory Be*☆

FIRST HEALING MYSTERY

The Healing of a Paralytic

☆*Our Father*☆

When Jesus returned to Capernaum . . . /

41

he preached the word to them.

Mark 2:1,2

☆*Hail Mary*☆

They came bringing to him a paralytic
    carried by four men. /
Unable to get near Jesus because of
    the crowd, they opened up the roof
    above him.

Mark 2:3-4

☆*Hail Mary*☆

After they had broken through, /
    they let down the mat on which the
    paralytic was lying.

Mark 2:4

☆*Hail Mary*☆

When Jesus saw their faith, he said to the
    paralytic, /
"Child, your sins are forgiven."

Mark 2:5

☆*Hail Mary*☆

Now some of the scribes were sitting
there asking themselves, /
"Why does this man speak that way?
He is blaspheming. Who but God
alone can forgive sins?"

Mark 2:6-7

☆*Hail Mary*☆

Jesus immediately knew in his mind
what they were thinking. . . . /
"Why are you thinking such things in
your hearts?"

Mark 2:8

☆*Hail Mary*☆

"Which is easier, to say to the paralytic,
'Your sins are forgiven,' /
or to say, 'Rise, pick up your mat and
walk'?"

Mark 2:9

☆*Hail Mary*☆

"But that you may know that the Son of
Man has authority to forgive sins

on earth" . . . /
"I say to you, rise, pick up your mat,
and go home."

Mark 2:10-11

☆Hail Mary☆

He rose, picked up his mat at once, /
and went away in the sight of
everyone.

Mark 2:12

☆Hail Mary☆

They were all astounded and glorified
God, saying /
"We have never seen anything like
this."

Mark 2:12

☆Hail Mary☆
☆Glory Be☆

SECOND HEALING MYSTERY

The Woman With a Hemorrhage

☆*Our Father*☆

There was a woman afflicted /
   with hemorrhages for twelve years.

Mark 5:25

☆*Hail Mary*☆

She had suffered greatly at the hands of
   many doctors and had spent all that
   she had. /
Yet she was not helped but only grew
   worse.

Mark 5:26

☆*Hail Mary*☆

She had heard about Jesus /
   and came up behind him in the crowd
   and touched his cloak.

Mark 5:27

☆*Hail Mary*☆

She said, "If I but touch his clothes, /
  I shall be cured."

Mark 5:28

☆Hail Mary☆

Immediately her flow of blood dried up. /
  She felt in her body that she was
    healed of her affliction.

Mark 5:29

☆Hail Mary☆

Jesus, aware at once that power had
    gone out from him, /
  turned around in the crowd and asked,
    "Who has touched my clothes?"

Mark 5:30

☆Hail Mary☆

But his disciples said to him, "You see
    how the crowd is pressing upon
    you, /
  and yet you ask, 'Who touched me?' "

Mark 5:31

☆Hail Mary☆

He looked around to see who had done
   it. /
The woman, realizing what had
   happened to her, approached in
   fear and trembling.

Mark 5:32-33

☆*Hail Mary*☆

She fell down before Jesus /
   and told him the whole truth.

Mark 5:33

☆*Hail Mary*☆

He said to her, "Daughter, your faith
   has saved you. /
Go in peace and be cured of your
   affliction."

Mark 5:34

☆*Hail Mary*☆
☆*Glory Be*☆

THIRD HEALING MYSTERY

The Man Born Blind

☆*Our Father*☆

As he passed by /
   he saw a man blind from birth.

John 9:1

☆*Hail Mary*☆

His disciples asked him, "Rabbi, who
   sinned, /
   this man or his parents, that he was
   born blind?"

John 9:2

☆*Hail Mary*☆

Jesus answered, "Neither he nor his
   parents sinned; /
   it is so that the works of God might be
   made visible through him."

John 9:3

☆*Hail Mary*☆

"We have to do the works of the one
  who sent me while it is day. /
Night is coming when no one can
  work."

John 9:4

☆*Hail Mary*☆

"While I am in the world, /
  I am the light of the world."

John 9:5

☆*Hail Mary*☆

When he had said this, he spat on the
  ground and made clay with the
  saliva, /
and smeared the clay on his eyes."

John 9:6

☆*Hail Mary*☆

[Jesus] said to him, "Go wash in the
  Pool of Siloam". . . . /
So he went and washed, and came
  back able to see.

John 9:7

49

☆*Hail Mary*☆

Jesus . . . said, "Do you believe in the
    Son of Man?" . . . /
    He said, "I do believe, Lord," and he
    worshiped him.

John 9:35,38

☆*Hail Mary*☆

Then Jesus said, "I came into this world
    for judgment, /
    so that those who do not see might see,
    and those who do see might become
    blind."

John 9:39

☆*Hail Mary*☆

"If you were blind, you would have no
    sin; /
    but now you are saying, 'We see,' so
    your sin remains."

John 9:41

☆*Hail Mary*☆
☆*Glory Be*☆

FOURTH HEALING MYSTERY

The Adulteress

☆*Our Father*☆

Early in the morning [Jesus] arrived
    again in the temple area, /
  and all the people started coming to
    him, and he sat down and taught
    them.

John 8:2

☆*Hail Mary*☆

Then the scribes and the Pharisees
    brought a woman who had been
    caught in adultery /
  and made her stand in the middle.

John 8:3

☆*Hail Mary*☆

They said to him, "Teacher, this woman
    was caught /

in the very act of committing adultery."

John 8:4

☆*Hail Mary*☆

"Now in the law, Moses commanded us to stone such women. /
So what do you say?"

John 8:5

☆*Hail Mary*☆

Jesus bent down /
and began to write on the ground with his finger.

John 8:6

☆*Hail Mary*☆

But when they continued asking him, he straightened up and said to them, /
"Let the one among you who is without sin be the first to throw a stone at her."

John 8:7

☆*Hail Mary*☆

Again he bent down /
    and wrote on the ground.

                        John 8:8

        ☆*Hail Mary*☆

And in response, they went away one by
    one, beginning with the elders. /
So he was left alone with the woman
    before him.

                        John 8:9

        ☆*Hail Mary*☆

"Woman, where are they? Has no one
    condemned you?" /
She replied, "No one, sir."

                     John 8:10-11

        ☆*Hail Mary*☆

Then Jesus said, "Neither do I condemn
    you. /
Go, [and] from now on do not sin any
    more."

                      John 8:11

        ☆*Hail Mary*☆
         ☆*Glory Be*☆

FIFTH HEALING MYSTERY

The Healing of a Boy With a Demon

☆*Our Father*☆

When they came to the crowd a man
    approached, knelt down before
    him, /
  and said, "Lord have pity on my
    son. . . ."

Matthew 17:14-15

☆*Hail Mary*☆

"He is a lunatic and suffers severely; /
  often he falls into fire, and often into
    water."

Matthew 17:15

☆*Hail Mary*☆

"I brought him to your disciples, /
  but they could not cure him."

Matthew 17:16

☆*Hail Mary*☆

"O faithless and perverse generation,
how long will I be with you? /
How long will I endure you? Bring
him here to me."

Matthew 17:17
☆*Hail Mary*☆

Jesus rebuked him and the demon came
out of him, /
and from that hour the boy was cured.

Matthew 17:18
☆*Hail Mary*☆

Then the disciples approached Jesus in
private and said, /
"Why could we not drive it out?"

Matthew 17:19
☆*Hail Mary*☆

He said to them, /
"Because of your little faith."

Matthew 17:20
☆*Hail Mary*☆

"I say to you, if you have faith the size of
a mustard seed, /
    you will say to this mountain, 'Move
    from here to there,' and it will
    move."

Matthew 17:20
☆*Hail Mary*☆

"Nothing will be impossible /
    for you."

Matthew 17:20
☆*Hail Mary*☆

You belong to God, children, and you
    have conquered them, /
    for the one who is in you is greater
    than the one who is in the world.

1 John 4:4

☆*Hail Mary*☆
☆*Glory Be*☆

FIRST EUCHARISTIC MYSTERY

Feeding of the Five Thousand

☆*Our Father*☆

[Jesus] withdrew in a boat to a deserted place by himself. /

The crowds heard of this and followed
him on foot from their towns.

Matthew 14:13

☆*Hail Mary*☆

When he disembarked and saw the vast
crowd, /
his heart was moved with pity for
them, and he cured their sick.

Matthew 14:14

☆*Hail Mary*☆

When it was evening, the disciples
approached him and said, "This is
a deserted place and it is already
late; /
dismiss the crowds so that they can go
to the villages and buy food for
themselves."

Matthew 14:15

☆*Hail Mary*☆

[Jesus] said to them, "There is no need
for them to go away; /

give them some food yourselves."
                    Matthew 14:16
            ☆*Hail Mary*☆

But they said to him, /
    "Five loaves and two fish are all we
        have here."
                    Matthew 14:17
            ☆*Hail Mary*☆

Then he said, "Bring them here to me," /
    and he ordered the crowds to sit down
        on the grass.
                    Matthew 14:18,19
            ☆*Hail Mary*☆

Taking the five loaves and the two fish,
        and looking up to heaven, /
    he said the blessing, broke the
        loaves. . . ."
                    Matthew 14:19
            ☆*Hail Mary*☆

[He] gave them to the disciples, /

who in turn gave them to the crowds.

Matthew 14:19

☆*Hail Mary*☆

They all ate and were satisfied, and they
picked up the fragments left over — /
twelve wicker baskets full.

Matthew 14:20

☆*Hail Mary*☆

Those who ate were about five thousand
men, /
not counting women and children.

Matthew 14:21

☆*Hail Mary*☆
☆*Glory Be*☆

SECOND EUCHARISTIC MYSTERY

The Bread of Life

☆*Our Father*☆

When they found him across the sea they
said to him, /
   "Rabbi, when did you get here?"

John 6:25

☆*Hail Mary*☆

"I say to you, you are looking for me not
because you saw signs /
but because you ate the loaves and
were filled."

John 6:26

☆*Hail Mary*☆

"Do not work for food that perishes but
for the food that endures for eternal
life, /
which the Son of Man will give you."

John 6:27

☆Hail Mary☆

So they said to him, "What can we do /
   to accomplish the works of God?"

                        John 6:28

☆Hail Mary☆

Jesus answered and said to them, /
   "This is the work of God, that you
     believe in the one he sent."

                        John 6:29

☆Hail Mary☆

"Amen, Amen, I say to you, it was not
     Moses who gave the bread from
     heaven; /
   my Father gives you the true bread
     from heaven."

                        John 6:32

☆Hail Mary☆

"For the bread of God is that which
   comes down from heaven /

and gives life to the world."

John 6:33

☆*Hail Mary*☆

"I am the bread of life; whoever comes
to me will never hunger, /
and whoever believes in me will never
thirst."

John 6:35

☆*Hail Mary*☆

"Everything that the Father gives me
will come to me, /
and I will not reject anyone who
comes to me. . . ."

John 6:37

☆*Hail Mary*☆

"For this is the will of my Father, that
everyone who sees the Son and
believes in him /
may have eternal life, and I shall raise
him [on] the last day."

John 6:40

☆*Hail Mary*☆
☆*Glory Be*☆

THIRD EUCHARISTIC MYSTERY

True Food and True Drink

☆ *Our Father* ☆

"Amen, amen, I say to you, whoever
    believes has eternal life. /
    I am the bread of life."

John 6:47-48

☆ *Hail Mary* ☆

"Your ancestors ate the manna in the
    desert, but they died; /
    this is the bread that comes down from
    heaven so that one may eat it and
    not die."

John 6:49-50

☆ *Hail Mary* ☆

"Whoever eats this bread will live
    forever; /
    and the bread that I will give is my

flesh for the life of the world."

John 6:51

☆*Hail Mary*☆

The Jews quarreled among themselves,
saying, /
  "How can this man give us [his] flesh
  to eat?"

John 6:52

☆*Hail Mary*☆

"Amen, amen, I say to you, unless you
eat the flesh of the Son of Man /
and drink his blood, you do not have
life within you."

John 6:53

☆*Hail Mary*☆

"Whoever eats my flesh and drinks my
blood has eternal life, /
and I will raise him on the last day."

John 6:54

☆*Hail Mary*☆

"For my flesh is true food, /
  and my blood is true drink."

John 6:55

☆*Hail Mary*☆

"Whoever eats my flesh and drinks my
    blood /
  remains in me and I in him."

John 6:56

☆*Hail Mary*☆

Then many disciples who were listening
    said, /
  "This saying is hard; who can accept
    it?"

John 6:60

☆*Hail Mary*☆

Simon Peter answered him, "Master, to
    whom shall we go? /
  You have the words of eternal life."

John 6:68

☆*Hail Mary*☆
☆*Glory Be*☆

FOURTH EUCHARISTIC MYSTERY

The Last Supper

☆*Our Father*☆

When the hour came, /
   he took his place at table with the
     apostles.

Luke 22:14

☆*Hail Mary*☆

He said to them, "I have eagerly desired /
   to eat this Passover with you before I
     suffer. . . ."

Luke 22:15

☆*Hail Mary*☆

"For, I tell you, I shall not eat it [again] /
   until there is fulfillment in the
     kingdom of God."

Luke 22:16

☆*Hail Mary*☆

Then he took a cup, gave thanks, and said, /
   "Take this and share it among yourselves. . . ."

Luke 22:17

☆*Hail Mary*☆

"For I tell you [that] from this time on I shall not drink /
   of the fruit of the vine until the kingdom of God comes."

Luke 22:18

☆*Hail Mary*☆

Then he took the bread, said the blessing, /
   broke it, and gave it to them. . . .

Luke 22:19

☆*Hail Mary*☆

"This is my body, which will be given for you; /
   do this in memory of me."

Luke 22:19

☆*Hail Mary*☆

And likewise the cup after they had
eaten, saying, /
   "This cup is the new covenant in my
blood, which will be shed for you."

Luke 22:20

☆*Hail Mary*☆

For from the rising of the sun, even to its
setting, /
   my name is great among the
nations. . . .

Malachi 1:11

☆*Hail Mary*☆

And everywhere they bring sacrifice to
my name /
   and a pure offering. . . .

Malachi 1:11

☆*Hail Mary*☆
☆*Glory Be*☆

FIFTH EUCHARISTIC MYSTERY

Body and Blood of Jesus

☆*Our Father*☆

The cup of blessing that we bless, /
   is it not a participation in the blood of
      Christ?

> 1 Corinthians 10:16
> ☆*Hail Mary*☆

The bread that we break, /
   is it not a participation in the body of
      Christ?

> 1 Corinthians 10:16
> ☆*Hail Mary*☆

Because the loaf of bread is one, we,
      though many, are one body, /
   for we all partake of the one loaf.

> 1 Corinthians 10:17
> ☆*Hail Mary*☆

Therefore whoever eats the bread or
 drinks the cup of the Lord
 unworthily /
will have to answer for the body and
 blood of the Lord.

1 Corinthians 11:27
☆*Hail Mary*☆

A person should examine himself, /
 and so eat the bread and drink the
 cup.

1 Corinthians 11:28
☆*Hail Mary*☆

For anyone who eats and drinks without
 discerning the body, /
eats and drinks judgment on himself.

1 Corinthians 11:29
☆*Hail Mary*☆

That is why many among you are ill and
 infirm, /
and a considerable number are dying.

1 Corinthians 11:30

☆*Hail Mary*☆

If we discerned ourselves, /
    we would not be under judgment. . . .

                 1 Corinthians 11:31
         ☆*Hail Mary*☆

But since we are judged by [the] Lord,
    we are being disciplined /
so that we may not be condemned
    along with the world.

                 1 Corinthians 11:32
         ☆*Hail Mary*☆

He took bread, said the blessing, broke
    it, and gave it to them. /
With that their eyes were opened and
    they recognized him. . . .

                 Luke 24:30-31
         ☆*Hail Mary*☆
         ☆*Glory Be*☆

FIRST SORROWFUL MYSTERY

The Agony in the Garden

☆*Our Father*☆

They came to a place named
Gethsemane, and he said to his

disciples, /
"Sit here while I pray."

Mark 14:32

☆*Hail Mary*☆

He took with him Peter, James, and
John, /
and began to be troubled and
distressed.

Mark 14:33

☆*Hail Mary*☆

Then he said to them, "My soul is
sorrowful even to death. /
Remain here and keep watch with
me."

Matthew 26:38

☆*Hail Mary*☆

He advanced a little /
and fell prostrate in prayer. . . .

Matthew 26:39

☆*Hail Mary*☆

"My Father, if it is possible let this cup
    pass from me; /
  yet, not as I will, but as you will."

Matthew 26:39

☆*Hail Mary*☆

And to strengthen him /
  an angel from heaven appeared to
    him.

Luke 22:43

☆*Hail Mary*☆

He was in such agony and he prayed so
    fervently that his sweat /
  became like drops of blood falling on
    the ground.

Luke 22:44

☆*Hail Mary*☆

When he returned he found them asleep.
    He said to Peter, /
  "Simon, are you asleep? Could you
    not keep watch for one hour?"

Mark 14:37

☆*Hail Mary*☆

"Watch and pray that you may not
      undergo the test. /
  The spirit is willing but the flesh is
      weak."

                        Mark 14:38

☆*Hail Mary*☆

"Get up, let us go. /
  See, my betrayer is at hand."

                        Mark 14:42

☆*Hail Mary*☆
☆*Glory Be*☆

SECOND SORROWFUL MYSTERY

The Scourging at the Pillar

☆*Our Father*☆

When it was morning . . . /
    They bound him, led him away, and
    handed him over to Pilate.

Matthew 27:1,2

☆*Hail Mary*☆

Pilate questioned him, "Are you the king
    of the Jews?" /
    He said to him in reply, "You say so."

Mark 15:2

☆*Hail Mary*☆

"My kingdom does not belong to this
    world. . . . /
    As it is, my kingdom is not here."

John 18:36

☆*Hail Mary*☆

"For this I was born and for this I came
into the world, to testify to the
truth. /
Everyone who belongs to the truth
listens to my voice."

John 18:37

☆*Hail Mary*☆

Pilate said, "I find no guilt in him. . . . /
Do you want me to release to you the
King of the Jews?"

John 18:38,39

☆*Hail Mary*☆

But they were adamant and said, "He is
inciting the people /
with his teaching throughout all
Judea. . . ."

Luke 23:5

☆*Hail Mary*☆

Pilate said, "No capital crime has been
committed by him. /
Therefore I shall have him flogged

and then release him."

Luke 23:15-16

☆*Hail Mary*☆

Then Pilate took Jesus /
and had him scourged.

John 19:1

☆*Hail Mary*☆

But he was pierced for our offenses, /
crushed for our sins. . . .

Isaiah 53:5

☆*Hail Mary*☆

Upon him was the chastisement that
    makes us whole, /
by his stripes we were healed.

Isaiah 53:5

☆*Hail Mary*☆
☆*Glory Be*☆

THIRD SORROWFUL MYSTERY

The Crowning With Thorns

☆*Our Father*☆

Then the soldiers of the governor took
    Jesus inside the praetorium /
  and gathered the whole cohort around
    him.

                        Matthew 27:27
             ☆*Hail Mary*☆

They stripped off his clothes /
  and threw a scarlet military cloak
    about him.

                        Matthew 27:28
             ☆*Hail Mary*☆

Weaving a crown out of thorns, they
    placed it on his head, /
  and a reed in his right hand.

                        Matthew 27:29
             ☆*Hail Mary*☆

And kneeling before him they mocked
     him, saying, /
  "Hail, King of the Jews!"

Matthew 27:29

☆Hail Mary☆

They spat upon him /
  and took the reed and kept striking
     him on the head.

Matthew 27:30

☆Hail Mary☆

Once more Pilate went out and said to
     them, /
  "Look, I am bringing him out to you,
    so that you may know that I find no
    guilt in him."

John 19:4

☆Hail Mary☆

So Jesus came out, wearing the crown of
     thorns /
  and the purple cloak.

John 19:5

☆*Hail Mary*☆

And he said to the Jews, "Behold, your king!" /
>They cried out, "Take him away, take him away! Crucify him!"

John 19:14-15

☆Hail Mary☆

Pilate said to them, "Shall I crucify your king?" /
>The chief priests answered, "We have no king but Caesar."

John 19:15

☆Hail Mary☆

Then he handed him over to them /
>to be crucified.

John 19:16

☆Hail Mary☆
☆Glory Be☆

FOURTH SORROWFUL MYSTERY

The Carrying of the Cross

☆*Our Father*☆

They stripped him of the cloak, dressed
   him in his own clothes, /
   and led him off to crucify him.

Matthew 27:31

☆*Hail Mary*☆

As they were going out, they met a
   Cyrenian named Simon; /
   this man they pressed into service to
   carry his cross.

Matthew 27:32

☆*Hail Mary*☆

A large crowd of people followed Jesus, /
   including many women who mourned
   and lamented him.

Luke 23:27

☆*Hail Mary*☆

Jesus turned to them and said,
"Daughters of Jerusalem, do not
weep for me; /
weep instead for yourselves and for
your children. . . ."

Luke 23:28

☆*Hail Mary*☆

"For if these things are done when the
wood is green /
what will happen when it is dry?"

Luke 23:31

☆*Hail Mary*☆

"If anyone wishes to come after me, he
must deny himself /
and take up his cross daily and follow
me."

Luke 9:23

☆*Hail Mary*☆

Though he was harshly treated, he
submitted /

and opened not his mouth. . . .

Isaiah 53:7

☆*Hail Mary*☆

Like a lamb led to the slaughter /
   or a sheep before the shearers, he was
      silent. . . .

Isaiah 53:7

☆*Hail Mary*☆

Oppressed and condemned, he was taken
      away, /
   and who would have thought any
      more of his destiny?

Isaiah 53:8

☆*Hail Mary*☆

And carrying the cross himself he went
      out to what is called the Place of the
      Skull, /
   in Hebrew, Golgotha.

John 19:17

☆*Hail Mary*☆
☆*Glory Be*☆

FIFTH SORROWFUL MYSTERY

The Crucifixion

☆*Our Father*☆

When they came to the place called the
 Skull, /
 they crucified him. . . .

Luke 23:33

☆*Hail Mary*☆

[Then Jesus said, /
 "Father, forgive them, they know not
 what they do."]

Luke 23:34

☆*Hail Mary*☆

And they placed over his head the
 written charge against him: /
 This is Jesus, the King of the Jews.

Matthew 27:37

☆*Hail Mary*☆

Those passing by reviled him,

shaking their heads and saying, /
"You who would destroy the temple
and rebuild it in three days, save
yourself, if you are the Son of
God. . . ."

Matthew 27:39-40

☆Hail Mary☆

When Jesus saw his mother and the
disciple there whom he loved, /
he said to his mother, "Woman,
behold, your son."

John 19:26

☆Hail Mary☆

Then he said to the disciple, /
"Behold, your mother."

John 19:27

☆Hail Mary☆

And about three o'clock Jesus cried out
in a loud voice . . . /
"My God, my God, why have you
forsaken me?"

Matthew 27:46; Psalm 22:2a

☆*Hail Mary*☆

"Father into your hands I commend my
     spirit"; /
  and when he had said this he breathed
     his last.

Luke 23:46

☆*Hail Mary*☆

When the centurion who stood facing
     him saw how he breathed his last he
     said, /
  "Truly this man was the Son of God!"

Mark 15:39

☆*Hail Mary*☆

Taking the body, Joseph wrapped it [in]
     clean linen and laid it in his new
     tomb. . . . /
  Then he rolled a hugh stone across the
     entrance to the tomb and departed.

Matthew 27:59

☆*Hail Mary*☆
☆*Glory Be*☆

FIRST CONSOLING MYSTERY

The Beatitudes

☆*Our Father*☆

"Blessed are the poor in spirit, /
  for theirs is the kingdom of heaven."

Matthew 5:3

☆*Hail Mary*☆

"Blessed are they who mourn, /
 for they will be comforted."

Matthew 5:4

☆*Hail Mary*☆

"Blessed are the meek, /
 for they will inherit the land."

Matthew 5:5

☆*Hail Mary*☆

"Blessed are they who hunger and thirst
 for righteousness, /
 for they will be satisfied."

Matthew 5:6

☆*Hail Mary*☆

"Blessed are the merciful, /
 for they will be shown mercy."

Matthew 5:7

☆*Hail Mary*☆

"Blessed are the clean of heart, /

for they will see God."

Matthew 5:8

☆*Hail Mary*☆

"Blessed are the peacemakers, /
  for they will be called children of
    God."

Matthew 5:9

☆*Hail Mary*☆

"Blessed are they who are persecuted for
    the sake of righteousness, /
  for theirs is the kingdom of heaven."

Matthew 5:10

☆*Hail Mary*☆

"Blessed are you when they insult you
    and persecute you /
  and utter every kind of evil against
    you [falsely] because of me."

Matthew 5:11

☆*Hail Mary*☆

"Rejoice and be glad, /

for your reward will be great in
    heaven."

            ☆*Hail Mary*☆
            ☆*Glory Be*☆

SECOND CONSOLING MYSTERY

Dependence on God

☆*Our Father*☆

"Do not worry about your life, what you
   will eat [or drink], /
  or about your body, what you will
   wear."

Matthew 6:25

☆*Hail Mary*☆

"Look at the birds in the sky; they do
   not sow or reap . . . /
  yet your heavenly Father feeds them.
   Are not you more important than
   they?"

Matthew 6:26

☆*Hail Mary*☆

"Can any of you by worrying /

add a single moment to your life-
    span?"
                        Matthew 6:27
        ☆*Hail Mary*☆

"Learn from the way the wild flowers
    grow. /
They do not work or spin."
                        Matthew 6:28
        ☆*Hail Mary*☆

"But I tell you not even Solomon in all
    his splendor /
was clothed like one of them."
                        Matthew 6:29
        ☆*Hail Mary*☆

"If God so clothes the grass of the field
    . . . /
will he not much more provide for
    you, O you of little faith?"
                        Matthew 6:30
        ☆*Hail Mary*☆

"All these things the pagans seek. /

Your heavenly Father knows that you
need them all."

Matthew 6:32

☆*Hail Mary*☆

"But seek first the kingdom [of God]
and his righteousness, /
and all these things will be given you
besides."

Matthew 6:33

☆*Hail Mary*☆

"Ask and it will be given to you; seek
and you will find; /
knock and the door will be opened to
you."

Matthew 7:7

☆*Hail Mary*☆

"Do not worry about tomorrow;
tomorrow will take care of itself. /
Sufficient for a day is its own evil."

Matthew 6:34

☆*Hail Mary*☆
☆*Glory Be*☆

THIRD CONSOLING MYSTERY

God's Children

☆*Our Father*☆

Now this is the message that we have
    heard from him and proclaim to
    you: /
  God is light, and in him there is no
    darkness at all.

1 John 1:5

☆*Hail Mary*☆

If we say, "We have fellowship with
    him," while we continue to walk in
    darkness, /
  we lie and do not act in truth.

1 John 1:6

☆*Hail Mary*☆

But if we walk in the light as he is in the
    light, then we have fellowship with
    one another, /

and the blood of his Son Jesus cleanses
us from all sin.

1 John 1:7

☆*Hail Mary*☆

If we say, "We are without sin," we
deceive ourselves, /
and the truth is not in us.

1 John 1:8

☆*Hail Mary*☆

If we acknowledge our sins, he is faithful
and just /
and will forgive our sins and cleanse us
from every wrongdoing.

1 John 1:9

☆*Hail Mary*☆

Do not love the world or the things of
the world. /
If anyone loves the world, the love of
the Father is not in him.

1 John 2:15

☆*Hail Mary*☆

Yet the world and its enticement are
    passing away. /
  But whoever does the will of God
    remains forever.

1 John 2:17

☆Hail Mary☆

Beloved, we are God's children now;
    what we shall be has not yet been
    revealed. /
  We do know that when it is revealed
    we shall be like him, for we shall see
    him as he is.

1 John 3:2

☆Hail Mary☆

Those who keep his commandments
    remain in him, and he in them, /
and the way we know that he remains
    in us is from the Spirit that he gave
    us.

1 John 3:24

☆Hail Mary☆

For whoever is begotten by God
conquers the world. /
And the victory that conquers the
world is our faith.

1 John 5:4

☆*Hail Mary*☆
☆*Glory Be*☆

FOURTH CONSOLING MYSTERY

The Raising of Lazarus

☆*Our Father*☆

Now a man was ill, Lazarus from
     Bethany, /
the village of Mary and her sister
     Martha.

John 11:1

☆*Hail Mary*☆

When Jesus heard this he said, "This
     illness is not to end in death, /
but is for the glory of God, that the
     Son of God may be glorified
     through it."

John 11:4

☆*Hail Mary*☆

When Jesus arrived, /
     he found that Lazarus had already

been in the tomb for four days.

John 11:17

☆*Hail Mary*☆

Martha said to Jesus, /
    "Lord if you had been here, my
    brother would not have died."

John 11:21

☆*Hail Mary*☆

Jesus told her, "I am the resurrection
    and the life; /
    whoever believes in me, even if he dies,
    will live . . ."

John 11:25

☆*Hail Mary*☆

"And everyone who lives and believes in
    me will never die. /
    Do you believe this?"

John 11:26

☆*Hail Mary*☆

So they took away the stone. And Jesus

raised his eyes and said, /
"Father, I thank you for hearing me."

John 11:41

☆*Hail Mary*☆

"I know that you always hear me; but
because of the crowd here I have
said this, /
that they may believe that you sent
me."

John 11:42

☆*Hail Mary*☆

And when he had said this, he cried out
in a loud voice, /
"Lazarus, come out!"

John 11:43

☆*Hail Mary*☆

The dead man came out, /
tied hand and foot with burial bands,
and his face was wrapped in a cloth.

John 11:44

☆*Hail Mary*☆
☆*Glory Be*☆

FIFTH CONSOLING MYSTERY

The Last Supper Discourse

☆*Our Father*☆

"Do not let your hearts be troubled. /
   You have faith in God; have faith also
   in me."

John 14:1

☆*Hail Mary*☆

"In my Father's house there are many
   dwelling places. /
If there were not, would I have told
   you that I am going to prepare a
   place for you?"

John 14:2

☆*Hail Mary*☆

"And if I go and prepare a place for you,
   I will come back again /
   and take you to myself, so that where I
   am you also may be."

John 14:3

☆*Hail Mary*☆

"I am the way and the truth and the life. /
No one comes to the Father except
through me."

John 14:6

☆*Hail Mary*☆

"And I will ask the Father, and he will
give you another Advocate to be
with you always, /
the Spirit of truth. . . ."

John 14:16-17

☆*Hail Mary*☆

"Whoever loves me will keep my word,
and my Father will love him, /
and we will come to him and make our
dwelling with him."

John 14:23

☆*Hail Mary*☆

"Peace I leave with you; my peace I give
to you. Not as the world gives do I

give it to you. /
Do not let your hearts be troubled or
afraid."

John 14:27

☆*Hail Mary*☆

"Amen, amen, I say to you, you will
weep and mourn, while the world
rejoices; /
you will grieve, but your grief will
become joy."

John 16:20

☆*Hail Mary*☆

"So you also are now in anguish. But I
will see you again, and your hearts
will rejoice, /
and no one will take your joy away
from you."

John 16:22

☆*Hail Mary*☆

"In the world you will have trouble,

but take courage, /
I have conquered the world."

John 16:33

☆*Hail Mary*☆
☆*Glory Be*☆

FIRST GLORIOUS MYSTERY

The Resurrection

☆*Our Father*☆

At daybreak on the first day of the week /
they took the spices they had prepared

and went to the tomb.

Luke 24:1

☆*Hail Mary*☆

And behold, there was a great
earthquake; for an angel of the
Lord descended from heaven, /
approached, rolled back the stone,
and sat upon it.

Matthew 28:2

☆*Hail Mary*☆

"Do not be afraid! I know that you are
seeking Jesus the crucified. /
He is not here . . ."

Matthew 28:5-6

☆*Hail Mary*☆

"For he has been raised just as he said. /
Come and see the place where he
lay. . . ."

Matthew 28:6

☆*Hail Mary*☆

Then they went away quickly from the

tomb, fearful yet overjoyed, /
and ran to announce this to his
disciples.

Matthew 28:8
☆*Hail Mary*☆

And behold, Jesus met them on their
way and greeted them. /
They approached, embraced his feet,
and did him homage.

Matthew 28:9
☆*Hail Mary*☆

Then Jesus said to them, "Do not be
afraid. Go tell my brothers to go to
Galilee, /
and there they will see me."

Matthew 28:10
☆*Hail Mary*☆

On the evening of that first day of the
week . . . /
Jesus came and stood in their midst

and said to them, "Peace be with you."

John 20:19

☆*Hail Mary*☆

When he had said this, /
  he showed them his hands and his side.

John 20:20

☆*Hail Mary*☆

The disciples rejoiced /
  when they saw the Lord.

John 20:20

☆*Hail Mary*☆
☆*Glory Be*☆

SECOND GLORIOUS MYSTERY

The Ascension

☆*Our Father*☆

He presented himself alive to them by
many proofs after he had suffered, /
appearing to them during forty days
and speaking about the kingdom of
God.

Acts 1:3

☆*Hail Mary*☆

Then he led them [out] as far as Bethany, /
raised his hands, and blessed them.

Luke 24:50

☆*Hail Mary*☆

Then Jesus approached and said to
them, /
"All power in heaven and on earth has
been given to me."

Matthew 28:18

"Go into the whole world /
    and proclaim the gospel to every
        creature."

Mark 16:15

☆*Hail Mary*☆

"Whoever believes and is baptized will
    be saved; /
whoever does not believe will be
    condemned."

Mark 16:16

☆*Hail Mary*☆

"And behold, I am with you always, /
    until the end of the age."

Matthew 28:20

☆*Hail Mary*☆

"You will receive power when the Holy
        Spirit comes upon you, /
and you will be my witnesses in
        Jerusalem, throughout Judea and

Samaria, and to the ends of the
earth."

Acts 1:8

☆*Hail Mary*☆

When he had said this, as they were
 looking on, /
  he was lifted up, and a cloud took him
   from their sight.

Acts 1:9

☆*Hail Mary*☆

So then the Lord Jesus, after he spoke to
 them, /
  was taken up into heaven and took his
   seat at the right hand of God.

Mark 16:19

☆*Hail Mary*☆

But they went forth and preached
 everywhere /
  while the Lord worked with them and

confirmed the word through
accompanying signs.

Mark 16:20

☆*Hail Mary*☆
☆*Glory Be*☆

THIRD GLORIOUS MYSTERY

The Descent of the Holy Spirit

☆*Our Father*☆

When the time for Pentecost was
    fulfilled, /
    they were all in one place together.

Acts 2:1

☆*Hail Mary*☆

And suddenly there came from the sky a
    noise like a strong driving wind, /
    and it filled the entire house in
    which they were.

Acts 2:2

☆*Hail Mary*☆

Then there appeared to them tongues as
    of fire, /
    which parted and came to rest on each
    one of them.

Acts 2:3

☆*Hail Mary*☆

And they were all filled with the holy
  Spirit /
  and began to speak in different
    tongues, as the Spirit enabled them
    to proclaim.

Acts 2:4

☆*Hail Mary*☆

Now there were devout Jews from every
  nation under heaven staying in
    Jerusalem. . . . /
  They were all astounded and
    bewildered, and said to one
    another, "What does this mean?"

Acts 2:5,12

☆*Hail Mary*☆

Peter stood up with the Eleven, raised his
  voice, and proclaimed to them, /
  ". . . this is what was spoken through
    the prophet Joel . . ."

Acts 2:14,16

☆*Hail Mary*☆

" 'It will come to pass in the last days,'
      God says, /
  'that I will pour out a portion of my
      spirit upon all flesh.' "

Acts 2:17

☆*Hail Mary*☆

"Exalted at the right hand of God, he
      received the promise of the Holy
      Spirit from the Father /
  and poured it forth, as you [both] see
      and hear."

Acts 2:33

☆*Hail Mary*☆

"Repent and be baptized, every one of
      you, in the name of Jesus Christ for
      the forgiveness of your sins; /
  and you will receive the gift of the
      Holy Spirit."

Acts 2:38

☆*Hail Mary*☆

"For the promise is made to you and to
     your children /
  and to all those far off, whomever the
  Lord our God will call."

Acts 2:39

☆*Hail Mary*☆
☆*Glory Be*☆

FOURTH GLORIOUS MYSTERY

The Assumption

☆*Our Father*☆

"Behold, my servant whom I have
    chosen, /
  my beloved in whom I delight. . . ."
        Matthew 12:18; cf. Isaiah 42:1
        ☆*Hail Mary*☆

Arise, my beloved, my beautiful one, /
  and come!

          Song of Songs 2:13
        ☆*Hail Mary*☆

You are all-beautiful my beloved, /
  and there is no blemish in you.
          Song of Songs 4:7
        ☆*Hail Mary*☆

"Amen, I say to you, /

today you will be with me in
Paradise.''

Luke 23:43

☆*Hail Mary*☆

"My soul proclaims the greatness of the
Lord; /
my spirit rejoices in God my savior."

Luke 1:46-47

☆*Hail Mary*☆

"And from my flesh I shall see God; /
my inmost being is consumed with
longing."

Job 19:26

☆*Hail Mary*☆

"The Mighty One has done great things
for me, /
and holy is his name."

Luke 1:49

☆*Hail Mary*☆

Then God's temple in heaven was

opened. . . . /
There were flashes of lightning,
   rumblings, and peals of
   thunder. . . .

Revelation 11:19
☆*Hail Mary*☆

For if we believe that Jesus died and
   rose, /
so too will God, through Jesus, bring
   with him those who have fallen
   asleep.

1 Thessalonians 4:14
☆*Hail Mary*☆

Thus we shall always be with the Lord. /
Therefore, console one another with
   these words.

1 Thessalonians 4:17-18
☆*Hail Mary*☆
☆*Glory Be*☆

FIFTH GLORIOUS MYSTERY

The Coronation

☆*Our Father*☆

A great sign appeared in the sky, a
    woman clothed with the sun, with
    the moon under her feet, /
and on her head a crown of twelve
    stars.

Revelation 12:1

☆Hail Mary☆

The woman herself . . . had a place
    prepared by God, /
that there she might be taken care of.

Revelation 12:6

☆Hail Mary☆

She brings him good, and not evil, /
    all the days of her life.

Proverbs 31:12

☆*Hail Mary*☆

She reaches out her hands to the poor, /
    and extends her arms to the needy.

                            Proverbs 31:20
☆*Hail Mary*☆

She is clothed with strength and
    dignity . . . /
    and on her tongue is kindly counsel.

                       Proverbs 31:25,26
☆*Hail Mary*☆

Her children rise up and praise her; . . . /
    the woman who fears the Lord is to be
    praised.

                       Proverbs 31:28,30
☆*Hail Mary*☆

Give her a reward of her labors, /
    and let her works praise her. . . .

                          Proverbs 31:31
☆*Hail Mary*☆

"I will give the victor the right to sit with
    me on my throne, /
  as I myself first won the victory and sit
  with my Father on his throne."

                           Revelation 3:21
                ☆*Hail Mary*☆

"Whoever exalts himself will be
    humbled; /
  but whoever humbles himself will be
  exalted."

                          Matthew 23:12
                ☆*Hail Mary*☆

"Remain faithful until death, /
  and I will give you the crown of life."

                          Revelation 2:10
                ☆*Hail Mary*☆
                  ☆*Glory Be*☆

Appendix A

Prayers of the Rosary

APOSTLES' CREED

I believe in God the Father almighty, Creator of heaven and earth; and in Jesus Christ, his only Son, our Lord; who was conceived by the Holy Spirit, born of the Virgin Mary; suffered under Pontius Pilate, was crucified, died, and was buried. He descended into hell; the third day he arose again from the dead. He ascended into heaven, and is seated at the right hand of God the Father almighty; from thence he shall come to judge the living and the dead. I believe in the Holy Spirit, the Holy Catholic Church, the Communion of Saints, the forgiveness of sins, the resurrection of the body, and live everlasting. Amen.

OUR FATHER

Our Father, who art in heaven, hallowed be they name, thy kingdom come, thy will be done, on earth as it is in heaven. Give us this day our daily bread, and forgive us our trespasses as we forgive those who trespass against us, and lead us not into temptation, but deliver us from evil. Amen.

HAIL MARY

Hail Mary, full of grace, the Lord is with thee; blessed art thou among women, and blessed is the fruit of thy womb, Jesus. Holy Mary, Mother of God, pray for us sinners, now and at the hour of our death. Amen.

GLORY BE

Glory be to the Father, and to the Son, and to the Holy Spirit; as it was in the beginning, is now, and ever shall be, world without end. Amen.

FATIMA PRAYER

O my Jesus, forgive us our sins, save us from the fires of hell, and lead all souls to heaven, especially those most in need of they mercy. [Commonly prayed after each Glory Be]

HAIL HOLY QUEEN

Hail Holy Queen, Mother of mercy! Hail, our life, our sweetness, and our hope! To you do we cry, poor banished children of Eve; to you do we send up our sighs, mourning and weeping in this valley of tears! Turn then, most gracious advocate, your eyes of mercy toward us; and after this, our exile, show unto us the blessed fruit of your womb, Jesus. O clement, O loving, O sweet Virgin Mary!

Appendix B

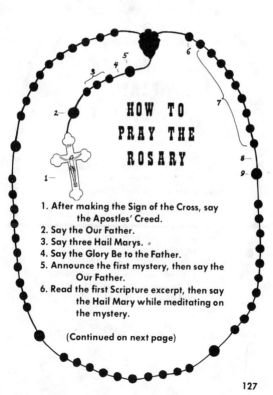

HOW TO PRAY THE ROSARY

1. After making the Sign of the Cross, say the Apostles' Creed.
2. Say the Our Father.
3. Say three Hail Marys.
4. Say the Glory Be to the Father.
5. Announce the first mystery, then say the Our Father.
6. Read the first Scripture excerpt, then say the Hail Mary while meditating on the mystery.

(Continued on next page)

HOW TO PRAY THE ROSARY

7. Repeat step 6 for the nine remaining Hail Marys in the decade.
8. Say the Glory Be to the Father.
9. Announce the second mystery, then say the Our Father. Repeat steps 6, 7, and 8 and continue with the third, fourth, and fifth mysteries in the same manner.
10. While not essential, it is very fitting to say the Hail Holy Queen at the end of the rosary, then kiss the cross and make the Sign of the Cross.